4/92

Creating with Soapstone

Strong coloration and rich texture of this Alaskan soapstone suit the bold contours of this stylized figure. The artist is Joel Queen, of Cherokee, North Carolina.

Kurt Haberstich

Creating with Soapstone

Simple Techniques, Beautiful Projects

Lark Books

I would like to thank my wife Ilse for her understanding and patience regarding the extensive activity I thought it necessary to devote to the completion of this book.

Sincere thanks also to Professor Hans-Rudolf Pfeifer of the Centre d'Analyse Minerale of the University in Lausanne for his expert support in reviewing the manuscript.

Translated from the German by Roswitha Friedl
Layout by Andreas D'Inca and Elaine Thompson
Photographs not credited on page 96 by Atelier Lightning

Library of Congress Cataloging-in-Publication Data
Haberstich, Kurt.
      [Gestalten mit Speckstein. English]
      Creating with soapstone : simple techniques, beautiful projects /
Kurt Haberstich ; [translated from the German by Roswitha Friedl].
         p.   cm.
      Includes index.
      ISBN 1-887374-13-2
      1. Soapstone carving--Technique.   I. Title.
      NK6058.H3313   1997

736'.5--dc20   96-28776
                                                                  CIP

Published by Lark Books
50 College Street
Asheville, NC 28801

English language text © Altamont Press 1997

Original text and illustrations © AT Verlag 1995

Originally published in Switzerland 1995 by AT Verlag

Distributed in the U.S. by Sterling Publishing,
   387 Park Avenue South, New York, NY 10016;
   1-800-367-9692

Distributed in Canada by Sterling Publishing,
   c/o Canadian Manda Group, One Atlantic Ave.,
   Suite 105, Toronto, Ontario M6K 3E7

Distributed in Great Britain and Europe by Cassell PLC,
   Wellington House, 125 Strand, London WC2R 0BB, England

Distributed in Australia by Capricorn Link (Australia) Pty Ltd.
   P.O. Box 6651, Baulkham Hills Business Centre, NSW 2153

Contents

Known worldwide for the sophistication of their carved figures, the Inuit people of Cape Dorset, in Canada's Northwest Territories, work with the distinctive local stone. Johnny Inukpuk carved Woman and Child *in 1954 of dark green stone and ivory. From the collection of the Canadian Museum of Civilization. Reproduced with permission of Lá Fédération des Coopératives du Nouveau-Québec, Baie D'Urfe, Quebec. Photo courtesy of the Inuit Art Information Centre, Hull, Quebec.*

Preface

Soapstone is an ideal material for sculpting. It is easy to shape, it comes in a variety of colors, textures, and forms, and it looks like marble when it is polished. Working with soapstone demands no knowledge of sculpture and requires no previous experience. Expensive tools are not needed, nor is extraordinary physical strength. Anyone who is willing to devote a little time and use a bit of sensitivity can create with this soft, silky-feeling material.

Working with soapstone can have a therapeutic effect. Analysis of the interior and exterior form of the stone, coupled with one's feelings for the stone and the design ideas the stone inspires, leads to an intense dialogue with the stone. This dialogue, in turn, soothes the spirit. It is not surprising that, in recent years, creative work with soapstone has been introduced in art and crafts classes, in schools and adult education courses, and in workshops for the disabled.

Enthusiasm for shaping and working with the stone comes not from imitating existing sculptures, but from one's own imagination. A sculpture, no matter what it means to others, always brings more joy when it was created from an original idea. With increasing skill and familiarity with materials and techniques, the sculptor gains confidence and develops freedom of expression. It is helpful to know about the various kinds of soapstone and the tools used to work it.

The first three chapters cover the necessary technical information. Following these chapters are numerous projects with detailed instructions, intended to familiarize you in the simplest way with the material and with shapes, and to inspire your own ideas. The projects are designed to encourage you to overcome any inhibitions about creating freely with soapstone. Finally, there is a gallery of photos that illustrate the variety of forms and textures that can come from soapstone, and that show inspiring examples from the work of contemporary artists.

Having said this, I hope your work will be exhilarating and creative. May every piece, guided by your feelings and shaped by your hands, become something you will treasure always.   —Kurt Haberstich

The Basics

What Is Soapstone?

The scientific name for soapstone is talc-chlorite slate, or steatite (from the Greek *stear* or *steatos*, meaning "grease"). It belongs to the family of greenstones. This crystalline-metamorphic rock consists largely of the minerals talc and chlorite, both of which contain magnesium and iron. In addition, soapstone may contain slightly harder minerals such as serpentine (dark green), carbonate (white or brownish), magnetite (black, metallic and shiny), pyrite ("cat's gold"), and rarely quartz (white or glassy looking).

The hardness and appearance of soapstone is determined by the mineral content. Soapstones rich in talc are the softest kinds; those with a high content of carbonate and serpentine are hard. In its fresh state it is mostly whitish or greenish gray. Contact with rainwater colors it brownish due to rust formation. Soapstone has a high specific gravity—approximately 3 grams per cubic centimeter—making it significantly heavier than most rocks. A fist-size piece weighs about 2.2 pounds.

There are few rocks that have been given as many names as steatite. Depending on the stone's use, it may be called soapstone, ovenstone, potstone, gold stone, seal stone, pipe stone, Comer stone, lavez stone (from the Italian *laveggio*, meaning "boiler"), *pietra ollare*, from the Latin *olla*, for "pot," *pierre tendre*, or "soft stone," and grease stone.

When polished, soapstone looks remarkably like genuine marble, yet it is among the softest of all solid minerals. On the Mohs scale, the standard hardness scale for minerals, talc is graded 1, with diamonds, the hardest mineral, numbered 10. Soapstone, which looks slightly greasy and feels silky, can be scraped with a fingernail and can be shaped with simple tools such as a knife, saw, rasp, or file.

Other highly valued characteristics are its fireproof quality and its ability to retain heat. Unlike other rocks which burst when exposed to high temperatures, soapstone lasts for decades without damage. Once heated up, it stays warm for

Work at a soapstone mine in the Swiss Alps, 7500 feet above sea level.

hours. Because of these qualities it was a much sought-after material for ovens, lamps, and cookware. Like other minerals, however, it is brittle. It can take stress only in the form of pressure, not tension; it is not resistant to blows, and it breaks when it is bent.

Soapstone exists almost everywhere in the world. It exhibits a wide variety of color schemes. The palette ranges from pure white to ivory, yellowish, light to dark green, pink, reddish, brown, light to dark gray, and even a charcoal gray. Often it is marbelized, speckled, streaked, or veined with other colors. In its raw and dry state, however, it is more or less white. The colors and patterns appear only when it is wet or polished.

For the use of sculpting, materials from Egypt, Australia, Brazil, China, India, and East Africa are among the most suitable. Soapstone found in Switzerland and Germany is often too hard for such work, and because of its popularity there, even the smaller deposits are mostly depleted.

Soapstone in History

Soapstone vessels and sculptures have been found all over the world, some dating back to 3000 B.C. This indicates that soapstone, together with alabaster, is one of the oldest rocks—possibly *the* oldest rock—used for utilitarian objects and sculptures. By the Stone Age, people had already learned to shape steatite with simple tools for many different purposes. Mesopotamians made it into drum-shaped roll seals. In the Indian Republic of Burma it was used as a pencil or stylus for writing on slate; in Asia it served as soap. African cultures mixed the ground stone meal into their foods.

Vessels made from soapstone were also used in Persia and in Greek cultures as long ago as 3000 B.C. Well-preserved vases and artifacts from this time are exhibited today in the museum of Heraklion on Crete.

According to discoveries in the United States, Canada, and India, we can assume that in these areas soapstone carving had its place in craftsmanship 400 to 500 years ago. The Inuit people, who used to use soapstone only for making oil lamps, are now well known for their excellent miniature sculptures. The Zuni of New Mexico have a long tradition of using soapstone or serpentine for their hunting fetishes. The Shona sculptures of Zimbabwe are of similar origin, and are still being produced for the tourist trade.

In Europe's Alpine regions, this soft, acid-resistant and fireproof material was traditionally used for pots, oil lamps, ovens, molds, and melting pots. Modern lifestyles have just about put an end to this centuries-old artisanry. Soapstone pieces have also been found in other locations—Peru, Egypt, Syria, and the Urals, to name a few—indicating the importance of soapstone in the past.

In recent times, people have become reacquainted with soapstone, and are learning again to appreciate its diverse qualities. It is used increasingly not just as an artistic medium, but for commercial purposes as well. We encounter the rock daily in the form of talcum powder, ointments and

make-up, toothpaste and pharmaceutics. It is used in grease and sealing material, insulation material, pest control substances, and for many other manufactured products.

It is also pleasant to note that in the past few years creating with soapstone has become popular in art and crafts classes, and as therapy in schools for the disabled.

Steatite vases from the Minoan culture (3000 to 2000 B.C.), showing historically important relief illustrations. From the museum in Heraklion, Crete.

Inca figurines made of gray-black soapstone, handmade in the Cuzco, Peru, area.

As recently as the beginning of this century, soapstone pots and pans were standard offerings at the market in Locarno, Switzerland.

Creating with Soapstone

Unlike modeling compounds like clay and polymers, where a shape is created by adding material, soapstone objects develop as layers are removed. Once the material has been removed, it cannot be put back. And unlike a painting, a sculpture is a three-dimensional object that has to be shaped all around and must be visually appealing from every side.

It is a good idea to start with easy shapes and progress step by step. Since raw soapstone is relatively inexpensive, a not-quite-successful attempt is not a great calamity. If you have removed too much material at one point or another, or if a splinter breaks off, it does not mean that the piece is ruined. With a little imagination it is still possible to create a pretty shape, perhaps a pendant or a hand-soothing rock. There really are no bad pieces.

No previous experience with stone work is required to shape soapstone. To create sculptures, however, it is helpful to be able to visualize in three dimensions and to be able to reduce figures to their essentials.

It is easier to allow the shape of the raw stone itself to dictate a design than to force a preconceived shape onto the stone. Although soapstone is easy to shape, every piece has its own character. It would not be appropriate, for example, to start with a raw piece that looks like a fish and try to make it into something different. This quality is an advantage more than a disadvantage. Not every creation has to has to be made according to a specific plan, nor does the original plan have to be followed through to the end. Many successful pieces have been created accidentally when the sculptor has simply followed the shape of the raw stone.

For a beginner, it is a good idea to work this way and to concentrate on shaping techniques rather than on a pre-planned design. This method will help develop familiarity with the tools and materials.

A drawing or sketch can be helpful when you want to create a specific form. The drawing need not be a masterpiece, but will serve as a guide to form and direction. A drawing will also help you gain an understanding of spatial relationships. Spatial thinking can be developed, too, if you try to recognize the shape of a sculpture or a rock by touch whenever possible. The sense of touch allows us to experience the shape much more intensely than is possible with the eye. If the touching is done with closed eyes, there are no visual distractions to interfere with concentration on the shape of the rock.

Observations in nature are also helpful. Every imaginable line and shape can be found somewhere in the natural world. When we experience nature with all senses alert, we find inspiration in blossoms, buds, leaves, birds, and animals that can easily be transferred to rock. It may also be helpful at first to try small practice pieces in geometric shapes.

As you can see, there are plenty of possibilities to train the sense of form. To close this chapter, here is a thought which may help overcome any mental obstacles.

Don't be afraid!

It is still
The creative spirit
Which
Invents ideas,
Decides the final shape
Or representation,
Guides hand and tool
Independent
Of the medium.

Significant
Is our courage and our creativity
Which we have to allow
To have enough freedom.

Materials and Tools

The Availability of Soapstone

Soapstone deposits are found in many countries and in most parts of North America. Every location produces rock with particular color and hardness characteristics.

It would be fun to get the raw material directly at the source of origin; however, many mines are on private property. Many are also located in relatively inaccessible places that can be dangerous to explore on one's own.

It is best to purchase easy-to-use soapstone in a craft store or from a specialty mail order supplier. These not only have an ample selection of soapstone in various colors but also have complete sets of tools. Check, too, with schools or instructors that offer courses in soapstone work; they will often have a decent selection of raw material and will sell it directly.

A Soapstone Sampler

Since most raw soapstone in its dry state has a whitish appearance, it is not always easy to recognize its true color. It is even more difficult to figure out the interior color and structure. It is usually possible only to guess, then hope for the best.

The following color charts show a selection of soapstone pieces in both the raw and polished states. The few examples are by no means a complete survey of soapstone; they are only meant to give an idea of the range of color tones and structures that are to be found.

White

This Brazilian stone is very soft.
It is sometimes almost pure white,
but more often marbleized light
gray. Small quartz stones may be
mixed in; they will not present a
problem when carving.

Ivory

This stone is from China. It may
have a slight yellowish tinge.
It occasionally shows hard spots
that mean higher risk of breakage
and have to be considered when
working small details.

19

Pink

Also from China, this soapstone sometimes has a milky, translucent appearance and may contain crystals and hard spots. It almost always is strongly veined. It is very soft and easy to shape.

Light green

Stone of this color is found in Brazil, China, India, Egypt, and elsewhere. It is very easy to use. The stone from China is slate-like, and can be split with a chisel. The layers have to be examined carefully because they present a breakage risk.

Dark green

The United States, India, and Finland produce stone this color, often with a blue or turquoise tint and with white inclusions. The Finnish and North Carolina stone of this color is quite hard and more difficult to shape.

Dark green speckled

From Switzerland, this multi-colored stone exhibits interesting coloration. It is usually very hard and better suited to machined work. Softer varieties with the same color characteristics can sometimes be found in craft stores.

Brown

Stone of this color, found in Brazil and parts of the United States, occasionally will include green or beige coloration. It sometimes has inclusions of varying degrees of hardness. It is compact and fissure free, an excellent stone for the beginner.

Black

This stone is actually charcoal gray with pale gray inclusions. It is compact, with very few fissures, and is usually harder than the lighter-colored stone. Because of the low risk of breakage it is very suitable for finer and more intricate carving. This piece is from China.

The Work Place

Working with soapstone produces great quantities of fine dust. During the warmer months, therefore, it is not only more pleasant but less messy to work outdoors. An indoor work room should be well ventilated and arranged so that stone dust can be cleaned away easily. It is better to vacuum up the dust; wiping just spreads it around. The work space should have optimal lighting.

Except for an occasional slip with the rasp, saw, or carving knife, working with soapstone poses relatively little danger. Leather gloves are a good precaution when working with the larger tools. Safety glasses should be worn to protect the eyes from dust and flying chips. Indoors, especially, a respirator or mask will guard against inhalation of stone dust.

For a work table, an old table or a board placed on cinder blocks or is adequate. A layer of plastic or paper, or rubber matting will make it easy to dispose of the accumulated stone meal; the latter also will keep the work piece from sliding. A wet cloth is also suitable as a work surface; it will help keep down the dust. Another alternative is to work directly over a plastic bowl which will catch the dust.

Some pieces are easier to hold if they are embedded in a "pillow" of sand on the tabletop. Smaller pieces can be worked in your lap; in this case, you may wish to wear an apron.

The Tools and Their Uses

Simple tools, those used for woodworking and those available in many households, are adequate for beginning soapstone work. Many diverse shapes can be created with a single tool. With a saw, half-round rasp, knife, sculptor's rasp, file brush, dry and wet sandpaper, a dust brush, and a small can of paste wax, even very intricate objects can be created. As you work with soapstone for a time, you probably find that a larger assortment of tools has accumulated almost on its own.

Experienced shapers of soapstone frequently use homemade and adapted tools, or tools designed for some other purpose. The tools illustrated are merely suggestions for a start-up assortment and not meant to exclude any personal favorites. What is important is that the tool you use is one with which you are familiar and which feels good in your hand.

The tools and accessories are listed and described in the typical order of their use.

For rough work

Hand saw (a), small hacksaw (b)

For the first steps of shaping the raw piece, the hand saw is very useful. The design of the blade is more important than the saw itself: most effective is a coarse-toothed, cross-cutting blade that will remove stone meal with both the push and pull strokes. A small hacksaw or frame saw with a removable blade is suitable for finer work: the modelmaker's saw, coping saw, jeweler's saw, and the like. For some jobs, you will want to use just the blade. Stone meal will clog a saw blade quickly and must be removed frequently. Always saw slowly and with light pressure.

Shaping tools

Hammer (c), Flat chisel (d), Straight edge chisel (e), Gouge chisel (f)

To split a raw piece or to remove edges, the flat chisel or the straight edge chisel is best; if these tools are not available, a wide screw driver or a flat piece of steel can be used instead. To remove uneven spots in rounded hollows, a gouge chisel is better.

Rasps (g)

Collectively, the teeth of a rasp are called the "cut." For rough shaping, half-round and round rasps are recommended. Wooden handles are more comfortable to use than plastic. Rasps can be purchased in various lengths. The tool should be comfortable to hold and of a size that is suitable for the piece that will be made. Work with rasps only on dry material; wet soapstone clogs the cut and causes rust.

Rasp ring (h)

Rasp rings, half-round rasps shaped into circles, are available in various sizes and are excellent for forming hollows and dips, as in bowls and sculptures. Instead of the ring, you can use a gouge (j), and create the hollow by chiseling or shaving.

Riffler rasps (i)

Not absolutely necessary, but riffler rasps are quite valuable for some shaping tasks. They are available in a wide assortment of shapes: round, half-round, rectangular, square, triangular, knife, spoon, lens, or oblong.

Files

When shaping soapstone, sandpaper can often be substituted for a file. Files often have criss-crossed cuts. Since the cuts are finer than those of rasps, less material is taken off per stroke, which also means that file work leaves finer scratch marks on the stone. Files are used, then, after rasps. The finer the cut of the file the more quickly it clogs with stone meal and the more frequently it will have to be cleaned. A file filled with stone dust is ineffective. As with rasps, files should not be used with wet material.

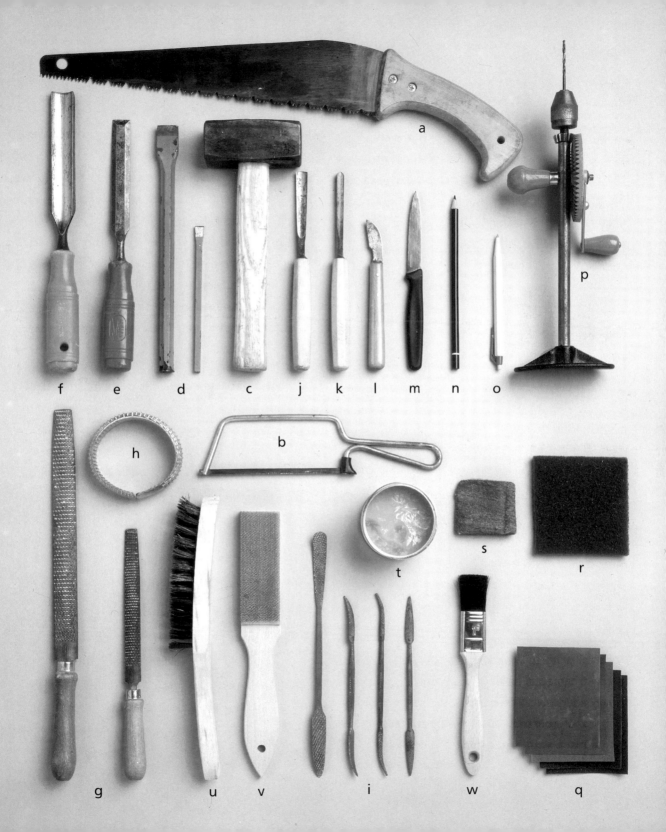

a

f e d c j k l m n o p

g u v i w q

h b t s r

Carving tools

Gouge (j), veiner tool (k), carving knife (l), paring knife (m)

Soapstone can be carved with any shorter knife that can be handled well. Old kitchen knives are just as suitable for certain types of work as gouging knives or linoleum tools. A blade dulls very quickly when working with stone, so you will need a sharpening stone. Always sharpen wet.

Drawing and etching tools

Charcoal pencil (n), ballpoint pen (o)

For drawing outlines of figurines, contours, etc., a charcoal pencil or a pointed nail is suitable. Felt tip pens will absorb the stone dust and become useless. To etch designs onto finished work, try an old ballpoint pen that has run out of ink. It handles easily, an asset when applying pressure for a length of time. In addition, the rounded tip will not catch at small dips or protrusions in the stone.

Drilling tools

Hand drill (p)

For smaller holes like those in jewelry, and even for larger ornamental holes in sculpture, a hand drill is usually adequate. A power drill with a small bit can be used, of course, if you have one. Conical holes can be made with a bodkin or a paring knife.

Sanding and polishing equipment

Dry and wet sandpaper (q), sanding cloth (r), steel wool (s)

Use dry sandpaper ranging in coarseness from 60 to 400 grit. For wet sanding, use grits of 400, 600, 800, and for the final smoothing, 1000 grit. Wet sandpaper remains usable for a long time, especially the fine grades.

Sanding cloth is synthetic and can be used for dry or wet sanding. It is available in coarse, medium and fine grit. Steel wool, grade 000, can be substituted for sandpaper for the final smoothing of a piece. The disadvantage is that it tends to rust.

Wax (t)

A final surface treatment will give the finished piece a smooth, silky shine, and bring out the color and pattern of the stone. Butcher's wax, paste wax, or even neutral shoe polish will work. Natural larch resin balsam, if available, is excellent. Rub wax over the piece, then buff it with a soft cloth.

Cleaning

Steel wire brush (u), file brush (v)

Special brushes are available to clean files and rasps; however, a conventional wire brush will work just as well.

Dust brush (w)

To prevent spreading dust unnecessarily around the room, stone dust should not be blown off the piece as you work, but brushed away gently.

Above: The powdery grayish surface of a piece of raw soapstone reveals little of the stone's true character.

Right: When a spot on the face of the stone is smoothed and polished, the stone comes to life, its rich color and texture now apparent.

Working with the Stone

Soapstone is not always compact; it is frequently veined and may contain bits of rough, harder minerals. The piece may break easily in an area of uneven hardness. In the raw stone or rough-hewn state, such hard spots cannot always be seen. For this reason, it is highly important to select the raw material carefully since it will determine the results. To get an idea of what the piece will look like when it is polished, wet the stone to bring out its color and pattern.

Despite the fact that soapstone is easy to work, even the smallest raw stone has its own distinctive character. The carver may not impose just any shape on a piece of stone. If you choose a raw stone only by looking at the color or the pattern, and fail to consider veins or badly joined layers, the piece may fall apart during the final steps of the shaping. This happens most often with free-standing parts such as handles, wings, arms, or legs. it is always best to choose a raw stone with a shape that coincides to some extent with the piece you have in mind.

Using the Raw Stone Form

For your first attempts, work with the inherent shape of the raw stone. Color and pattern play a minor role. First, try in your mind to transfer a suitable form or figure onto the raw stone. To make it easier, draw the raw stone shape on a piece of paper and sketch the approximate contours of the desired shape on top of it.

The photographs illustrate the way in which the shape of a raw stone is integrated into the design and transformed into the finished pieces.

1 In the raw stones, the carver sees a bird and a fish.

2 The shape of the raw stone is drawn on paper, then the planned finished shape superimposed upon it.

3 Rough shaping has been done with a half-round rasp.

4 The pieces have been sanded to their final shapes.

5 The finished sculptures: the bird rests on a base of contrasting raw stone; the fish is mounted with a pole on a polished base.

2

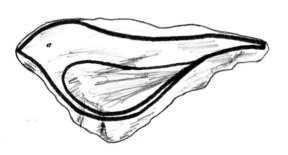

3

2

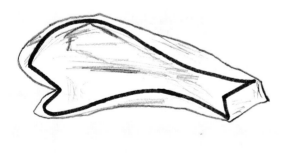

3

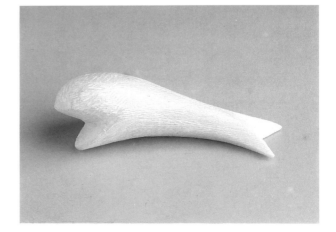

4

5

4

5

When the bird was shaped, close attention was paid to the proportions. The head, body, tightly aligned wings, and the tail should have accurate proportions. The lively effect created by the white pattern in the stone was a lucky accident. The soapstone base for the sculpture was left rough and unshaped to provide the greatest possible contrast to the polished figure. The bird was flattened on the bottom surface so it could be set on any surface. It could be glued to its base with a special stone glue.

With the fish, the most prominent characteristic of the raw stone was shaped into the gaping mouth that gave the figure its distinctive look. Since there was no way to represent water, the fish was placed on a translucent plastic pole. This gives it the impression of weightlessness and evokes the gliding movement through water. The soapstone base was prepared and polished; then a hole the size of the pole was drilled into the bottom of the fish and in the top of the base. The pole was glued into both pieces.

For both figures, bird and fish, we used a small, half-round rasp for the rough shaping and dry sandpaper with grits 60 and 180 for the fine shaping. Sandpaper grits 400, 600, and 1000 were used for wet sanding, the final step in smoothing the figure. The bird's eye was carved with a pointed knife and was scraped out again after the balsam polishing process so its matte finish would stand out against the polished surface.

It makes sense for beginners especially to take inspiration from the given forms and structures of raw stone pieces. The prominent lines then only have to be accentuated: carved out, shaped, and completed.

Shaping the Raw Stone

When you cannot find a suitable piece of raw stone of the shape you have in mind, one can be cut from a larger stone or split off with hammer and chisel. As an alternative, a large stone often can be split by dropping it onto a hard surface. The stone will break where it is weakened by veins, cracks, or infusions—an advantage in that the resulting pieces will present fewer unpleasant surprises when they are worked.

The photographs illustrate the typical process of shaping soapstone, and show how the tools are handled.

Using Soapstone Meal

A great quantity of soapstone dust, or meal, can be produced during the process of shaping. This waste is an excellent natural garden fertilizer. Simply sprinkle the meal around the plants and work it into the soil. It also helps keep snails and slugs away; they cannot glide over the dust since it sticks to their undersides.

1

4

1 Use a handsaw for the initial shaping of moderately large raw stones. Saw to the desired size and rough contours; create a standing surface.

2 For this bowl, rough shaping is done with a rough rasp.

3 The hollow is created with a gouge.

4 A rasp ring is used to further shape the hollow.

5 The shape of the hollow is refined with a riffler rasp.

2

3

5

6

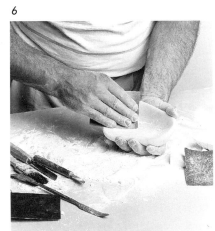

7

6 The piece is wet-sanded with increasingly fine paper, working from 400- to 1000-grit.

7 A dry sanding cloth or 000 steel wool could be used instead.

8 A surface finish of neutral hard wax is applied and the piece buffed with a soft cloth.

9 The finished bowl.

8

9

Repairing Broken Pieces

Don't panic when something breaks! Broken pieces or pieces that splinter because of harder inclusions or veins are not necessarily ruined. Usually it is easy to glue broken soapstone back together. Glue made specifically for stone work will make a permanent repair. Once the glue is thoroughly dry, the area can be sanded, if necessary, and polished. With careful work, the repair will hardly be visible.

The window picture shown at right broke during dry sanding because veining in the stone was not considered when the stone was selected. On page 49 is a photo of the broken window picture invisibly glued—a successful finished piece. Breaks in intricate pieces like this often can be prevented if work is done with the piece lying on a flat surface.

Ornaments and Jewelry

A Popular Piece for Beginners: the Hand Soother

As a first experience with soapstone, it is best to start with a fairly small piece left over from a larger one. Choose a stone that can just be grasped in the hand to make sure that the finished stone will not be too small, but will lie comfortably in the palm of the hand nicely and can be turned easily. To make a simple hand soother more special, provide it with a custom-made tray.

Hand Soother

1 Remove all bothersome unevenness and edges from the raw soapstone piece with a rasp.

2 Sand and polish the stone until it lies in the palm of your hand nicely.

Tray

1 Use a piece of soapstone about the size of your fist. With a gouge or a bent riffler rasp, shape a hollow so that the hand soother sits neatly in it.

2 Sand and polish the hollow. The outer contours can be left raw or finished smoothly, whichever you prefer.

Custom Jewelry
At Affordable Prices

Handmade soapstone jewelry is equally popular with children and adults. An original pendant, medallion, brooch, or necklace is relatively easy to make and uses very little material. Splinters or leftovers from larger objects are very suitable, and they can be purchased inexpensively in craft stores.

Necklace with Round and Oval beads

Making a beautiful bead necklace is not difficult, but it requires some patience. The smaller the work piece, the harder it is to hold onto while you are working. Be careful not to drop the beads onto a stone floor or any other hard surface; they can break easily at the veins. Keep the size of the beads fairly small so that the completed necklace will not be too heavy and cumbersome.

1 For each bead, saw off a rectangular piece of stone measuring ⅜ inch by ⅜ inch by 1 inch or longer. The longer the rectangle, the easier it is to hold in the hand.

2 With a rasp, shape the rectangle into an octagon and then into a round bar. The edges could also be rounded with a knife. Shape one end into the desired round or oval form, also with a rasp.

3 Saw off the pre-shaped end piece to the desired length.

4 Use the rasp to round the cut end to the rough finished shape.

5 Use a bodkin or a pointed knife to start the hole through the bead. Make a small indentation in each end of the bead.

6 With a hand or elecric drill, carefully drill the hole through the bead, making it approximately $1/16$ inch in diameter. Drill from each end to the center. If children are making the beads, an adult should drill the holes.

7 Sand the beads with dry sandpaper (grits 60 and 180), then wet-sand, going from rough to fine grit paper.

8 According to your preference, wax or polish the beads, or leave them unpolished.

9 String the beads onto a length of cord or thin leather.

Pendant

1 Saw a slice of stone approximately $1/8$ inch thick and slightly larger than the desired finished size of the pendant, or select a suitable splinter piece.

2 Scratch the desired design onto the plate with a nail or draw it on with a charcoal pencil.

3 Cut the exterior shapes using a fine-toothed saw.

4 Pre-drill the hole for the hanging cord, or carefully scratch it out with a pointed knife.

5 Carefully drill the hole with a $1/16$-inch bit. Because of the risk of breakage with delicate pieces like this, the holes should be drilled, if possible, at the beginning, before the piece has been worked too much.

6 Clean the hole and round its edges with rasp and knife.

7 Sand the raw form, first dry and then wet, going from coarse to fine sandpaper.

8 Wax and polish the piece.

9 String onto a cord or leather thong.

Floral Pin

1 Prepare a soapstone slice approximately 2¾ inches square and ⅜ inch thick.

2 Draw the flower shape onto the piece with a charcoal pencil or nail.

3 Saw out the contours with a fine-toothed saw. Round off the edges toward the back side with a rasp or a knife.

4 Carve out the petals on the front with a gouge or pointed riffler rasp and round the center with a knife.

5 Sand the raw form with dry, then wet, sandpaper, going from coarse to fine grit.

6 Glue pin back (available at craft stores) onto the upper third of the back. Let it dry completely.

7 Wax and polish the pin.

Window Pictures

When light shines through paler-colored soapstone, it highlights the veins and patterns to enhance the pictures. These pieces are nice miniature statues too, with the bottom flattened to provide a sturdy base, or with a separate base glued to the bottom.

Remember, there is a danger of breakage when working on delicate pieces like these, especially if the stone is sliced thinly. Take care to position the central figure in such a way that it is connected to the frame in at least three places.

As an alternative to the rectangular frame, try a round, oval, multi-sided or irregularly shaped frame. Sometimes interesting effects can be obtained by working in the negative—leaving the outer frame solid and cutting away a central motif.

Window Picture

1 Begin with a soapstone slice approximately 3 inches by 4½ inches.

2 Either draw the frame and the motif directly onto the stone, or draw a paper template and trace around it onto the stone.

3 To saw out the interior, drill ⅛-inch holes at the inner corners at the points where the frame meets the motif as shown in the illustration on page 48.

4 Pull a coping saw blade through the holes and saw out the spaces. Because of the risk of breakage, work with the plate lying flat on a surface. Saw slowly and with very little pressure. A modelmaker's saw blade could be used instead, in which case the holes would have to be drilled slightly larger.

5 Smooth the contours with a small rasp, a knife, or a wooden stick wrapped in sandpaper.

6 Sand the raw shape, first dry then wet, going

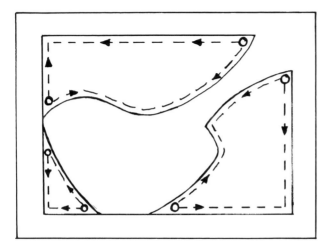

from coarse to fine paper.

7 Wax and polish the piece.

8 Attach a chain, cord, or leather band as shown to hang the window picture.

Etching and Relief Drawing

By the early part of the Stone Age, people had already learned to express themselves artistically. They left us a chronicle in stone: etched drawings, paintings, and reliefs. Their techniques were well developed, their workmanship perfect, and their art most impressive in the richness of its representations.

Today, many artists work with high and low reliefs. Soapstone is an ideal medium for such representations, since subjects with simple contours are relatively easy to transfer onto the material. Unlike free-standing sculpture, the pictorial design of a relief is attached to a surface. By rounding the edges of the design, the picture is given a three-dimensional effect.

Flat Relief Picture

1 Begin with a thick stone slice, purchased ready-made or cut from a larger piece. It should have one natural, uncut side onto which the relief will be worked. For a different effect, use a piece that has been cut on both sides. So that the piece will stand upright like the one in the photograph, saw the stone straight across the lower edge and smooth the surface with a rasp and file.

2 Draw the motif contours onto the stone with a charcoal pencil or chalk, or scratch them in with a pointed nail or bodkin. If you find it easier, make a paper template and use it to mark the design onto the stone. Carve the contours into the stone with a knife, making the cuts about $1/16$ to $1/8$ inch deep.

3 With a knife, gouge, or riffler rasp, shave out the motif. Leave the center portion slightly higher and shave the edges slightly lower to create a three-dimensional effect.

4 Dry- and wet-sand the relief picture, working with increasingly fine grit paper, so that the picture stands out from the surface of the raw stone.

5 Depending on the chosen motif or the function, wax and polish the relief.

For a high relief design, the process is reversed. Material around the motif is removed and the area polished, with the motif itself rough and unpolished.

While a relief is somewhat rustic in appearance, etching produces a more delicate design and a rather refined finished piece.

Etched Stone

1 Cut a thickness of stone to the desired size. Drill a hole for hanging, if desired, approximately $\frac{1}{16}$ inch in diameter. As an alternative, cut and smooth one surface to stand the piece upright as shown in the photograph.

2 Sand and polish the stone on one, two or all sides.

3 Make a stencil for the design, if desired. Copy the motif onto the polished stone with a charcoal pencil. The design may also be drawn directly on the plate.

4 It is best to use an old ballpoint pen, without ink, to etch the drawn motif into the stone to the desired depth. Pointed drawing tools like a drawing compass are more suitable for adding texture or refining lines.

5 Use a brush to remove the dust from the etching. To hang it, pull a cord or leather thong through the hole.

The rose etching shown in the photograph was worked on the back of the fish relief. This practice not only saves materials, but makes for variety. With a 180-degree turn, the work of art can be converted to suit the occasion.

Statuettes

A variety of techniques can be used, singly or in combination, to make small statues and standing pictures: carving, etching, shaping, sawing, and adding attached pieces. A separate cut motif can be glued behind a window, or a motif can be cut as a single piece with the window as was described on page 47.

Statue with Flying Gulls

A smooth, polished stone provides the background for a trio of birds in flight. The attached figures can be the same color or different colors, as long as they contrast well with the background to produce the best effect. Contrast can also be textural, with the background left in the raw state or sanded but unpolished, and the figures polished to a high gloss, or the other way around.

To make the background, prepare the stone as described for the etched stone on page 52. Make the figures according to the instructions for the floral pin on page 46. To reduce the risk of break-

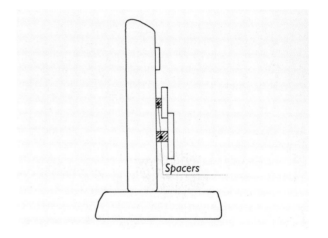

Spacers

age, avoid cutting the stone slices too thin.

The birds are affixed to the background with varying spacing to give the piece more life. The upper one is attached directly to the background; the lower two are glued in place with spacers of two different lengths as shown above.

Statues should be steady on their feet and should not tip easily. If the background piece does not have an adequate standing surface, a separate base can be glued to it. The base might be made of the same or contrasting stone, or of wood, metal, or Plexiglas.

Practical Pieces from Soapstone

Desk Accessories

To make practical pieces intended for daily use—from accessories for the desk and dining table to candleholders and holiday ornaments—soapstone is an appropriate and diversified medium. The high specific gravity of the stone, more of a disadvantage for delicate pieces like jewelry, is an asset for household objects since it gives them a certain sturdiness and stability.

Penholder and Photo Stand

If you want to make a penholder with a minimal investment of time and effort, start with a raw stone that is an appropriate size and shape for the project. Then it is only necessary to sand the surface smooth and bore the holes.

Drill holes approximately ½ inch wide and 1½ inches deep. Widen them slightly at the top with a knife, or counterbore with a larger drill bit. Polish the stone, if desired, or leave it in the natural state.

If a suitable raw stone is not available, it takes just a bit more time to saw a piece from larger stone and shape it to your liking.

For the photo or postcard stand, also try to start with a raw stone of a suitable size and shape. As an alternative, cut a piece from a large stone, but try to cut to a natural-looking shape. The size of the piece will depend upon the photos or cards that will be displayed.

Saw the slot at an angle of approximately 75 degrees so that the photo will lean slightly toward

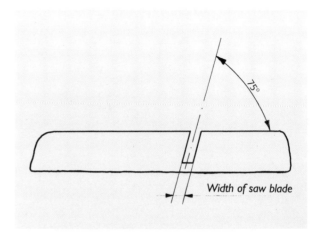

Width of saw blade

the back. Make the cut two-thirds of the way through the base as shown in the sketch. Polish the piece, if you wish. A beautiful raw stone can be as attractive as one that has been highly polished.

Pen Tray

So that the tray will serve you well, it is important that the pens can be removed and put in place with ease. A workable spacing for the grooves is approximately 1 inch from center to center; the depth

should be approximately ¼ inch, as shown in the drawing. The angled pen tray shown on page 61 is planned well, keeping pens neatly within reach.

We started with a larger raw stone and sawed a wedge approximately 4¼ inches square. In thickness, it tapers from approximately 1½ inches to ¾ inch.

Make four grooves the whole length of the surface, using the half-round side of a rough rasp. Round the edges on all sides with the rasp and coarse sandpaper. Sand smooth with finer sandpaper, then polish the piece.

Memo or Card Holder

For cards, photos, notepaper, and other such things a U-shaped tray is very handy. Select a stone that is to your liking. It can be a piece of raw stone that is a good size for the project, or a piece cut from a larger stone.

There are several ways to create the inner U shape. With method 1, illustrated on the next

Method 1

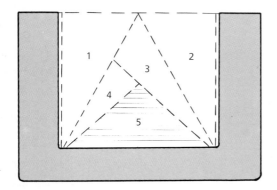

Method 2

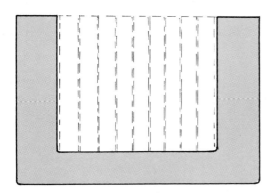

page, cuts are made to remove wedge-shaped pieces (steps 1 through 4). If the cuts do not meet at the corners, the pieces can be broken out.

The remaining triangle (5) is removed with a rasp, working parallel to the base surface.

In method 2, make cuts approximately ¼ inch apart to the same point at the base. The single slices then can be broken out and the surface evened with a rasp. Then all edges are rounded, and the piece sanded and polished.

The material can also be removed using just the rasp, but this is a more difficult and time-consuming method. For an attractive finishing touch, the exterior side surfaces might be decorated with etched motifs.

Paperweight

A useful paperweight need not be any specific size or shape, which makes it a good project for beginners. It can, of course, be shaped to your ideal design with the investment of a little more time and effort. Let your imagination reign, and create a piece that suits your ability and taste.

Candleholders and Christmas Ornaments

Candleholders made from soapstone are particularly well-suited for tea lights. The recessed holder prevents the candle from falling out when it has burned away. As an extra safety precaution, the base can be made wider than the top of the holder to reduce the chances of it tipping over.

Candleholder

1 To provide a good, flat base, it is best to saw a piece from a larger raw stone.

2 Plan the placement of the hole so that one side of it will be at the highest point on the stone.

3 Drill a hole approximately ½ inch in diameter. The hole should be approximately 1 inch deep for wax candles; about ¾ inch deep for a tea light.

4 Enlarge the hole to the desired candle diameter with a knife and rasp.

5 For a tea light, smooth out the inner surface of the hole with a gouge. Use a rasp and file to even the bottom of the base.

6 Sand and polish the candleholder.

It is worth a try to sand and polish just certain areas on the piece. With some spots left natural, the piece will have a more rustic look. Try, too, using a larger stone for a holder to accommodate several candles.

The angel and Christmas tree star are relatively small pieces. They were shaped from flat pieces of stone, yet they seem three-dimensional. The effect is achieved by rounding all edges well, and by accenting features like wings, arms, and folds in the clothing by carving into the surface. Color and pattern of the soapstone also contribute tremendously to the finished appearance.

With a charcoal pencil, draw each shape on a ⅜-inch thick slice of stone, or use a stencil. Saw around the marked lines with a fine-toothed saw or coping saw. Sand smooth. Polish, if desired, or leave the piece natural. Add the accents with an old ball-point pen or a nail.

For a standing figurine, add a base if necessary to keep the figure upright. To make a tree ornament, drill a small hole at the top to insert a cord for hanging.

Cookie cutters were used as templates to make both the figures shown. One of the angel's wings suffered a break while work was in progress, but after careful gluing and sanding, it's as good as new.

Bookends and Vases

Soapstone is an excellent material for these pieces; its weight and density are definite advantages. The side of each bookend that faces the books should be at a right angle to the base surface so the pair will support the books correctly. To help keep the bookends in place, glue a sheet of slip-resistant rubber to the base of each. The rest of the shape is up to your imagination.

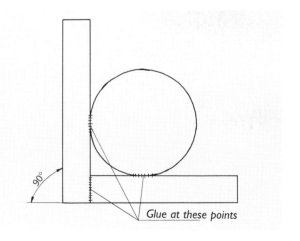

90°

Glue at these points

Bis die gute Zeit anbricht

BESINNLICHKEIT

Für diesen Augenblick

Es wäre so...

Der Schäfer

Weg-Gedanken

Gedichte und Aphorismen

Gedanken zum Sein

Gedichte und Aphorismen

Kurt Haberstich

Kurt Haberstich

Kurt Haberstich

Kurt Haberstich

Erzählung

Kurt Haberstich

Der
Schäfer

Bookends can also be assembled from smaller components, as shown in the drawing on page 64. For this design, cut and shape two pieces of stone approximately 4 inches square and ⅝ inch thick. Glue the pieces together at a right angle. While the glue is hardening, make a ball, a cone, or any shape you like. This piece will later be glued into the open angle to add reinforcement and weight. Sand the angle, then glue the third piece in place. Polish the bookends.

A very simple pair of bookends can be made in next to no time. Choose two attractive raw stones, each weighing approximately four pounds. Saw or shave two adjacent right-angled surfaces on each piece and the rustic-looking book supports are complete.

Small Vase

1 Saw a piece of stone approximately 2½ by 2½ by 4 inches. The dimensions may vary, but the base must be square.

2 Using a ¹⁄₁₆-inch bit, drill a hole from the center of the top to about 1 inch above the bottom. Always drill without applying pressure and remove the dust frequently to prevent damage to the stone.

3 Shape the exterior according to your own design, possibly first by sawing, then using the rasp and coarser sandpaper to fine-tune the shape.

4 Enlarge the opening with a round file, knife, or a wooden stick wrapped in sandpaper, and shape it conically.

5 Work the bottom surface so it is perfectly flat.

6 Sand the vase smooth, and polish it.

7 If you wish, embellish the exterior surface by etching a design or motif.

To Dress Up the Dining Table

Objects in everyday life should offer aesthetic pleasure in addition to performing their practical functions. They can be serviceable and still contribute to the beautification of daily routine.

A practical characteristic of soapstone is that it stays cool even in a warm room. In some rural areas of the world, soapstone containers are still used to store and preserve foods such as butter and lard.

The dimensions given in the instructions are those used for pieces shown in the photographs. Alter them, if you wish, to suit your own requirements.

Coasters and Napkin Rings

Octagonal Coaster

1 Cut seven stone slices 2 inches square and ⅜ inch thick. Use any combination of colors.

2 With a rasp and file, trim all the slices to the same size, making sure all edges are at right angles.

3 Cut two plates in half diagonally to make four triangles.

4 Arrange the five squares in a pleasing pattern and glue them together in a cross shape on a paper surface. Let the piece dry.

5 Place two triangles of the same color into opposite corners and repeat with the other two, to create an octagonal shape.

6 Glue them in place and let the glue dry completely.

7 Remove the paper and work the top and bottom surfaces with rasp and file until they are flat and smooth.

8 Sand the contours and round the edges with 100-grit sandpaper.

9 Sand and polish the coaster.

10 If desired, glue a thin piece of felt or cardboard to the bottom.

Individual Coasters

Make them round or square, add an etched design or an inlaid motif—let your imagination run wild. The only caveat is to keep the coasters rather thin; ⅜ inch is a good thickness. If they are too thick, they look rather clumsy, and it is too easy to chip a fragile glass by knocking it against the coaster's edge.

The two coasters illustrated are approximately 3½ inches in diameter and ⅜ inch thick. The central insets in both were fitted into openings that had been sawed out and filed. They were then glued in place. After the glue hardened, both sides were sanded and polished.

Napkin Rings

1 For each napkin ring, saw out a piece of soapstone with the approximate dimensions of the planned shape.

2 Draw the outline of the shape on paper, or scratch it directly onto the stone. Determine placement for a hole approximately 1½ inches in diameter.

3 Using a hand drill or electric drill and small bit, drill through the stone at the planned point.

4 Enlarge the hole with a knife or rasp, smoothing the edges.

5 Finish shaping the piece according to your plan.

6 Sand, working from coarser to finer paper, and polish.

Condiment Dish

The useful bowl, shown upper left in the photograph, is 4 inches in diameter at the top; 2½ inches at the bottom. It is 2 inches high. We begin with

a stone block approximately 4¼ by 4¼ by 2¼ inches. The procedure for making the bowl is described on pages 36 and 37.

Honey Pot

The Roman historian Pliny the Elder wrote in the year 70 A.D. about the existence of a green stone in the province of Como, "which is mined and turned into vessels, for use in preparation of foods and dishes." From this we can assume that soapstone containers were already being made on a lathe in ancient times.

It will become apparent with this project that concave inner spaces are more laborious to form than are outer covex surfaces. Use a little patience, and you will have a handmade vessel of which you can be very proud.

1 For the pot, begin with a block of fairly soft raw stone, 4 by 4 by 5 inches.

2 For the lid, saw a 1½-inch slice from one end of the stone.

3 On one end (the top) of the larger stone piece, draw three concentric circles as indicated in drawing 1, with diameters of 4 inches, 3 inches, and 2½ inches.

4 On a ⅜-inch metal drill bit, mark a point 2½ inches from the tip. Drill holes 2½ inches deep around the inner marked line, then drill a pattern of holes inside this ring as illustrated.

5 With the blade of a modeller saw, cut through the ribs that have been created, cutting first on the marked line. Make a a temporary handle for the blade by wrapping an end with tape.

6 Using a gouge, knife, small chisel, or screwdriver, remove the sawed ribs carefully, without applying too much pressure. The individual ribs may also be broken off with needlenose pliers, using only slight pressure.

7 With the same tools, shape out the interior of the pot down to the end of the drill holes. Round out the interior wall with a rasp and 60-grit sandpaper, and even the inner bottom surface with a gouge.

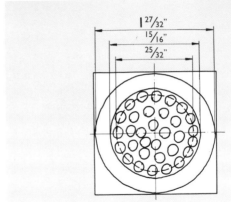

1

8 Shape the outside. Saw off the four corners to create an octagonally shaped pillar. Round the form with a rasp.

9 Make the bottom surface flat and even.

10 Sand the pot, working with coarser, then finer sandpaper. Polish the piece.

The Lid

Use the measurements in drawing 2 to shape the lid. Sand it as you did the pot, then polish it.

Soapstone containers used to hold foods should always be sanded smooth and polished for reasons of hygiene. When waxing, only use natural, non-toxic hard wax.

2

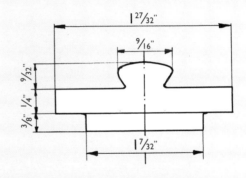

3

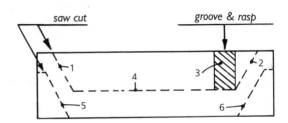

saw cut   groove & rasp

Butter Dish

A soapstone plate provides an attractive and unusual way to serve butter, cheese, or appetizers. Foods stay fresh longer on stoneware, too.

1 Prepare a stone slice 8 inches by 4 inches by 1½ inches.

2 Approximately 1¼ inches in from each end, make a cut ⅝ inches deep at a 30-degree angle, according to lines 1 and 2 in drawing 3.

3 With the rasp, make a vertical cut at each end, ⅜ inch wide and extending to the points of the first cuts as shown by the shaded area (3) on the drawing.

4 With a saw blade, cut away the material between the previous cuts to create the bottom of the dish—line 4 in the drawing.

5 With a saw, cut along lines 5 and 6 at the ends to remove the wedge-shaped pieces.

6 With a rasp, even out all rough spots from sawing, and smooth the bottom surfaces. Round off the ends as shown in the photograph.

7 Use sandpaper, perhaps with a sanding block, to even the bottom surface.

8 Sand the whole piece with increasingly fine paper, and polish.

Knife Rest

The individual knife rest at each place is an elegant accessory in the European tradition. For each, cut a piece of stone approximately 1¼ by 1¼ by 2⅜ inches. Shape a triangle at each end with a rasp. From the center, remove a piece about 1¼ inches long and ⅝ inch thick. (Use the photograph for reference.) Finish the piece by sanding and polishing.

An Assortment of Projects

Making a Sphere

Craftspeople working in all sorts of media consider a sphere to be one of the most difficult shapes to achieve with hand tools alone. This project presents a challenge, and is rewarding in several ways. For one, shaping a round object provides excellent training for the eye. The soothing feel of the ball in your hand as you shape it is a reward in itself. And as your sense of touch becomes attuned to the shape, you will begin to notice even the slightest rough or uneven spot.

The spheres, made to your most exacting standards, are unusual decorative accessories and pleasant as hand soothers. They are not, unfortunately, useful in games as the stone can shatter easily if it strikes a harder object or is dropped.

For the finished ball shown on page 77 we began with a 2½-inch stone cube weighing approximately 1¼ pounds. The completed ball was 2¼ inches in diameter and weighed only about 9½ ounces. That means that during the work process more than half the material was removed.

1 Saw a cube approximately 2½ inches on a side.

2 With the charcoal pencil or pointed nail, draw a circle about 2 inches in diameter on two opposite sides.

3 Use the saw to remove the four corners of one marked side and then the other, cutting them at a 45-degree angle. Saw off the newly made corners evenly until you have a multi-sided piece with surfaces that are nearly even in size. Always remember that when you start with a cube you have to remove the same amount of material on each surface in order to ensure that the ball will be perfectly round.

4 With the rasp, remove material from the newly created edges. It is a good idea to wear a glove on the hand that holds the ball to avoid injury in case there is a slip of the rasp. Roll the ball around in your hand, then roll it over a smooth surface to detect uneven spots. Keep working on the piece until it rolls smoothly.

5 Remove small uneven spots with 60-grit dry sandpaper.

6 Crunch up 120-grit dry sandpaper to make it soft and pliable, then hold it in the palm of one hand. Place the ball into the hand with the sandpaper, holding the ball with the fingertips, and turn the ball to sand it smooth. Loosen or tighten the grip as necessary. Every now and then, check the sphere for roundness by carefully feeling its surface.

7 For the final sanding, use wet sandpaper of 400, 600, and 1000 grit as described in step 6.

8 Wax and polish the sphere.

Simple Human Figures

The aesthetics of the human body have for centuries inspired creations in three-dimensional art. In contemporary work, some of the most well known, lifelike soapstone figures are those made by the Inuit people, especially those showing hunters and fishermen practicing their professions. The essential goal for the Inuit artist is to create a figure that is most realistic in its resemblance to the model. This does not mean that every sculptor must make figures that are anatomically precise in their representation of the human figure. The Inuit pieces, however, are excellent as examples of the portrayal of proportions, body postures, and movement of the human figure.

It is a worthwhile exercise to study illustrations of the human figure, then to practice sketching bodies at rest, and to observe bodies in motion and try to capture the movement on paper. Then comes the practical test. . . .

In sculpture, very simply made human figures, singly and in groups, standing, sitting, crouching or lying down, can be just as effective as figures that are anatomically correct down to the last detail.

Shapes from Nature and Geometric Shapes

Soapstone is as well suited to flowing, natural shapes as to precise geometric designs. A rigidly designed piece, with straight lines and angles, usually will be created from a definite plan. An abstract piece usually develops during the work process, following the direction of the stone itself and utilizing the stone's essential character.

A Gallery of Soapstone Pieces

Four contemporary pieces illustrate the diversity of color and texture to be found in soapstone from different geographic locations. The artists who created these pieces are members of Eastern Band of Cherokee Indians, and work through the Qualla Arts and Crafts Mutual in western North Carolina. The eagle, at left, was carved by carved by Joel Queen. The tall stylized figure is the work of Freeman Owle. The snake and the fetish at right are by John Julius Wilnoty.

An aspect of Cherokee tradition is illustrated through this carving of a woman grinding corn, by Lloyd Owle.

The artist can often see the face in a piece of raw stone. This expressive one was created by James Sneed, a member of the Eastern Band of Cherokee Indians. The stone is Alaskan.

In every part of the world, local wildlife provides an unending source of subject matter for area artisans. The lion and elephant above are from the Kisii district of Kenya.

At right, western North Carolina artist Dale Weiler has created a river otter afloat on a darker stone base. The wood frame defines the piece and provides textural contrast, while adding stability at the same time.

The rough-hewn turtle shape reveals no hint of the colors and markings to be found in the stone's interior. The finished turtle rests on a rock in its pond, the water's surface beautifully depicted by the pattern of the darker stone.

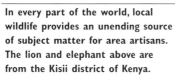

Soapstone and pipestone—which is different in mineral content but also easy to shape—were used by many North American tribes to make ceremonial pipes.

The pipe bowl at left is made of steatite and is four inches long. It is said to have belonged to Oglala Sioux Chief Crazy Horse. Photograph courtesy of The National Museum of the American Indian/Smithsonian Institution, negative number 39483.

This modern rendition of a traditional Cherokee pipe was made by John Julius Wilnoty.

Soapstone candlesticks can be designed simply or intricately to suit any level of carving skill. Above left, gracefully shaped Kisii stone figures perform a traditional Kenyan harvest dance. At right, flower petals, also of Kisii stone, are a popular motif for candleholders.

The cleverly designed two-piece candleholder can accommodate a range of candle sizes. Each side of the cube-shaped insert has a hole of a different diameter. The insert can be turned so the desired hole faces outward, then it is fitted snugly into the outer cube. The stone is Indian and is known locally as "Gorara" stone. In the Agra area, descendents of the marble carvers who built the Taj Mahal now apply their skills to making functional and ornamental objects from soapstone.

A hollow interior form is one of the most challenging to achieve. The bowl and vase, smooth and symmetrical, were shaped using only hand tools—and the experienced eye of the artisan. Both pieces are of Kenyan Kisii stone.

The lighter shades of Kisii soapstone are well suited to dyeing and etching. Spots were added to the cat at left with a paintbrush and dye. The cat at right was dipped into dye after its final sanding, then the details incised with a sharp knife point. The plates exhibit a combination of the two techniques; the central figure and colored motifs around the edge were painted with dye and the details etched with a knife.

Originally, natural plant dyes were used to color the soapstone. Readily available commercial dyes are used now, but most artists keep to the traditional colors.

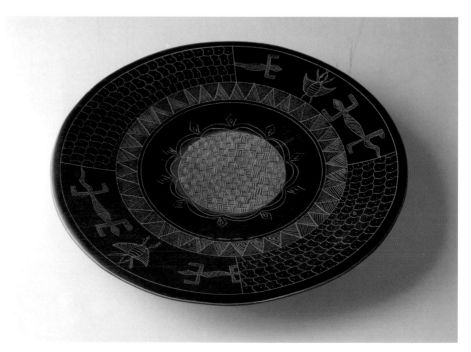

Strong colors in bold patterns provide the perfect accent for the stylized lines of the cat and the smooth contours of the bowl. Etched outlines separate and define the colors.

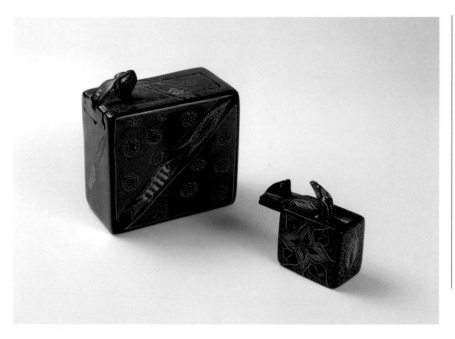

Traditional "snake boxes" illustrate a popular Kenyan tale: A mother frog decides to fight back against the snake that has repeatedly eaten her young. She painstakingly constructs a box with a sliding lid. She unhappily sacrifices one more baby, placing it in the box to lure the snake. When the snake enters the box she snaps the lid closed and jumps on top, where still she sits, guarding against the snake's escape.

Each box is carefully crafted so that when the lid slides open, the snake's head—attached with cord to the underside of the lid—appears to threaten the frog. The boxes are often dyed and and decorated with incised designs.

Part of the joy in working with soapstone is the excitement of discovering each stone's distinctive pattern and coloration as the powdery surface is smoothed away.

The snails—an especially pleasant shape to create—are of Indian stone, one with an unusual color combination. The vase, also from India, is richly colored stone speckled with milky translucent inclusions.

Novice or expert, every carver has an equal chance at uncovering a beautiful stone. Rob Pulleyn's first attempt at soapstone work revealed this handsomely patterned piece.

The Ballerina, by Dale Weiler, is elegantly styled in Argentinean stone. Watercolors were used to tint the costume and hair, and the piece was finished with urethane for a satin finish and for durability.

Soapstone adapts well to the lines and contours of the human figure. *Kneeling Man*, in the characteristic green stone of Baffin Island, was carved in 1987 by Kiawak Ashoona. Reproduced with permission of the West Baffin Eskimo Co-operative Ltd., Cape Dorset, NWT. Photo courtesy of Canadian Museum of Civilization, Hull, Quebec.

Artist Dale Weiler finds the greenish-brown speckled Argentinean soapstone perfectly suited to the aquatic wildlife he enjoys creating.

Above, an Atlantic salmon considers taking a lure, its delicate fins almost rippling with the current. The long body of the moray eel, right, is hidden from view in a cave of driftwood.

Fine or thin areas, like the fins of the salmon and teeth of the moray, present a challenge for even an experienced stoneworker. If the stone has weak areas resulting from inclusions or striations of other minerals, it can easily break at these points.

This extraordinary piece of stone from western North Carolina has an opalescent quality highlighted by bands of darker-colored mineral. Carving the small salamander's fine features from such a stone demanded great care and patience of the artist, Dale Weiler.

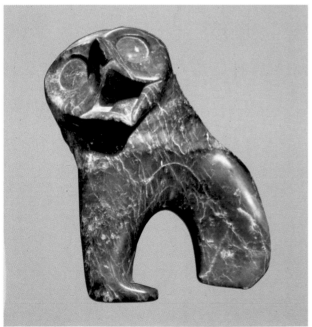

Osuitok Ipeelee's *Falcon* was carved from dark and light green Arctic stone in about 1982. Reproduced with the permission of the West Baffin Eskimo Co-operative Ltd., Cape Dorset, NWT. Photo courtesy of Canadian Museum of Civilization, Hull, Quebec.

Acknowledgements

A special thank you to the artists whose work appears on the preceding pages. Works not listed below were created by the author.

Joel Queen, pages 2, 83

Johnny Inukpuk, page 6

Freeman Owle, page 83

John Julius Wilnoty, pages 83 and 87

Lloyd Owle, page 84

James Sneed, page 84

Dale Weiler, pages 86, 93, 94, 95, and back cover

Rob Pulleyn, 92

Osuitok Ipeelee, page 95

. . . and the soapstone crafters of Tabaka, Kenya and of India's Agra district, whose names we do not know.

We also wish to express our gratitude to the following organizations that support working artists or that have provided photographs for this book:

Evan Bracken, Light Reflections, for the photographs on pages 2, 27, 83, 84 (lower), 85, 86, 87 (lower), 88-92, 93 (upper), 94, 95 (upper), and the back cover.

Originelle African Artifacts, Berkeley, California, for the gracious loan for photography of the Kenyan work on pages 85, 86, 88-91.

Qualla Arts & Crafts Mutual, the crafts cooperative of the Eastern Band of the Cherokee Indian, for their kind permission to photograph the pieces shown on pages 2, 83, 84, and 87.

World Market Place, retail stores representing SELFHELP Crafts of the World, for the kind loan of Kenyan and Indian soapstone pieces for the photographs on pages 88 (lower) and 92.

Canadian Museum of Civilization, Hull, Quebec.

Dorset Fine Arts, Division of West Baffin Eskimo Co-operative Ltd., Toronto.

Lá Fédération des Coopératives du Nouveau-Québec, Baie D'Urfe, Quebec.

The National Museum of the American Indian / Smithsonian Institution.

The Inuit Art Information Centre, Hull, Quebec.

The Colburn Gem & Mineral Museum, Asheville, North Carolina for their valuable technical assistance.

Index